HEINEMANN

UPPER LEVEL

Series Editor: John M

D1339926

Readers at *Upper Level* are intended as an aid to students which will start them on the road to reading unsimplified books in the whole range of English literature. At the same time, the content and language of the Readers at Upper Level is carefully controlled with the following main features:

Information Control   As at other levels in the series, information which is vital to the development of a story is carefully presented in the text and then reinforced through the *Points for Understanding* section. Some background references may be unfamiliar to students, but these are explained in the text and in notes in the *Glossary*. Care is taken with pronoun reference.

Structure Control   Students can expect to meet those structures covered in any basic English Course. Particularly difficult structures, such as complex nominal groups and embedded clauses are used sparingly. Clauses and phrases within sentences are carefully balanced and sentence length is limited to a maximum of four clauses in nearly all cases.

Vocabulary Control   At Upper Level, there is a basic vocabulary of approximately 2,200 words. At the same time students are given the opportunity to meet new words, including some simple idiomatic and figurative English usages which are clearly defined in the *Glossary*.

MAGHERAFELT COLLEGE
OF FURTHER EDUCATION

Guided Readers at Upper Level

HEINEMANN GUIDED READERS
ELEMENTARY LEVEL

ELECHI AMADI

The Great Ponds

Heinemann International
A division of Heinemann Educational Books Ltd
Halley Court, Jordan Hill, Oxford OX2 8EJ

OXFORD LONDON EDINBURGH
MELBOURNE SYDNEY AUCKLAND
SINGAPORE MADRID IBADAN
NAIROBI GABORONE HARARE
KINGSTON PORTSMOUTH (NH)

ISBN 0 435 27026 5

© Elechi Amadi 1969
First published 1969

This retold version for Heinemann Guided Readers
© John Davey 1976

This version first published 1976
Reprinted 1983, 1984, 1985 (twice), 1986, 1987, 1989

Cover photograph by George Hallett

Printed and bound by
Richard Clay Ltd, Bungay, Suffolk

Contents

Glossary

The glossary at the back of this book is divided into five sections. A number beside a word in the text, like this, [3] refers to a section of the glossary. The words within each section are listed in alphabetical order. Section 1 – comparisons – begins with a note on similes and then gives a list of those used in the text. Section 2 – terms to do with magic and religion – begins with a note on 'swearing an oath'. The page number given beside a word in the glossary refers to its first occurrence in the text.

Section 1 – comparisons
Section 2 – terms to do with magic and religion
Section 3 – terms to do with local life and customs
Section 4 – terms expressing emotion through body movements
Section 5 – general

The people in this story

In Chiolu

Eze Diali – the Chief of Chiolu
Chituru ⎱
Wezume ⎰ – elders of the tribe
Olumba – a warrior
Ikechi – a young man – a friend of Olumba
Nyoma – Olumba's first wife
Wogari – Olumba's second wife
Oda – Olumba's youngest wife
Nchelem – son of Olumba and Oda
Chisa – Eze Diali's daughter – loved by Ikechi
Ihunda – young daughter of Eze Diali

In Aliakoro

Eze Okehi – the Chief of Aliakoro
Wago (the Leopard-killer) – a warrior
Igwu – the dibia of the tribe
Okasi – a warrior

In Isiali

Elendu – a warrior

In Abii

Anwuanwu – the dibia of the tribe, working for the Chiolu

ONE
THE MEETING AT CHIOLU

Olumba lived in Chiolu – a small village in Eastern Nigeria. The people who lived there belonged to the Erekwi clan.[3] There were many ponds full of fish in the forests near Chiolu. The ponds were important to the villagers because they needed the fish for food.

One day Olumba was sitting in his hut mending some fish-traps.[5] He was sitting with his back to the door thinking about his work.

Ikechi, Olumba's friend, came into the compound[3] and walked very quietly towards Olumba.

'Why don't you sit down, Ikechi?' said Olumba suddenly without turning round.

'How did you know it was me?' replied Ikechi.

'I know the sound of your footsteps, don't I?' answered Olumba.

'But I didn't make any noise,' said Ikechi.

'Ha! Ha!' laughed Olumba. 'You think you didn't make a sound, but you made as much noise as an elephant.[1] You young men still have to learn to walk quietly.'

Ikechi sat down. 'What time is the meeting?' he asked.

'After the midday meal,' replied Olumba. 'Have you eaten anything yet?'

'No, I haven't,' replied Ikechi. 'I didn't feel hungry.'

'Are you excited?' asked Olumba.

'Not very much.'

'I think you are,' said Olumba. 'You hope you are going to fight. A man who is going to fight must eat first. If your stomach is empty, you will fight like an old woman. Come and eat some food with me. If you don't eat, you can't come with us.'

After the meal, Olumba picked up his matchet[3] and the two men walked slowly to the Chief's house. Olumba was a short man but he was strong. When he was young he had been a very good wrestler.[5]

Eze Diali, the Chief of the village of Chiolu, was sitting in his reception hall. The old men, or elders, came in and each one took a three-legged chair from a rail on the wall. The elders sat down around Eze Diali. The young men sat at the other end of the hall.

'People of Chiolu,' said the Chief, Eze Diali, 'we have heard that poachers[5] from the next village of Aliakoro will go to the Great Ponds tonight. These men will want to steal fish from the Pond of Wagaba. The Pond of Wagaba is full of fish and it belongs to us.'

Eze Diali looked round at the men who sat in silence. Then he continued.

'Tonight,' he said, 'we must capture some of these poachers and bring them back to Chiolu. Then we can sell these thieves back to their own village. If we capture some of these poachers, then perhaps the men of Aliakoro will stop stealing fish from our ponds. We want seven men to go to the Ponds tonight. And we must choose a leader.'

'Eze Diali,' said one of the old men, 'we don't want to spend a lot of time choosing a leader. Olumba is the strongest man. He is the best leader.'

Everyone agreed that Olumba should lead the men that night.

'We still need six men,' the Chief said again.

'I think Olumba should choose the six men he wants to take with him,' said another man. 'Olumba knows the young men well.'

'I agree,' said Eze Diali. 'Olumba, choose your six men and tell them what to do. I hope that tomorrow morning we shall have two prisoners captured from Aliakoro.'

Olumba chose the six men. One of them was his friend Ikechi. Olumba told the men his plans for the visit to the Great Ponds.

Later on, Olumba walked home and mended some more fish-traps. The men waited for the night to come before they set out on the journey.

TWO
THE POACHERS

When it was dark, the men of Chiolu met together and started on their journey to the Great Ponds. They walked through the big forests. The tall trees grew very close together and their branches joined overhead. It was like walking through a dark tunnel. But the men knew the paths well. And they were happy that it was so dark because nobody could see them.

The seven men reached the beginning of the ponds.

'We will go to the pond of Wagaba on the rafts,'5 said Olumba. 'How many rafts are there?'

'There are three rafts,' replied one of the men.

Olumba divided the men into three groups. They climbed on to the rafts and paddled quickly across the ponds until they reached the Pond of Wagaba.

The Pond of Wagaba was very large and no trees grew in it. But some of the trees on the edge of the pond had long branches, and these branches met over the middle of the pond. The moon shone through the branches.

The men sat on the rafts at the edge of the Pond of Wagaba and waited. The rafts were hidden under the low branches of the trees.

Suddenly one of the men whispered, 'Some men are coming.'

The poachers came on two rafts. They were talking quietly.

'I feel cold tonight,' one of the poachers said.

'You'll feel warmer when you see your trap full of fish,' replied another man.

Two other men laughed. Olumba listened carefully. He guessed that there were only four men on the two rafts.

One of the poachers said, 'I've never seen a pond with so many fish in it.'

'I wish it belonged to Aliakoro,' said another man.

'It may belong to us one day.'

'Why do you say that?'

'Eze Okehi, our Chief, wants it to belong to Aliakoro. He says the pond belongs to us and not to Chiolu.'

'But we'll have to fight for it to get it back,' said one of the poachers.

'The pond's worth fighting for, isn't it?' said another.

'It should . . .' The poacher's voice was drowned by a loud cry from Olumba. Olumba's men jumped off the rafts into the water. They attacked the men from Aliakoro. The men from Chiolu and the men from Aliakoro struggled, shouted and fought each other in the water.

Olumba struggled for a long time with one very strong man, but in the end he caught him.

'How many men have you captured?' Olumba asked his men.

'I have one man,' replied Ikechi.

'I have two,' said another.

'So we have three men altogether,' said Olumba.

'Let's go home now. Put the prisoners on the rafts.'

When they were on the rafts, Olumba spoke to the man he had captured.

'One of your men escaped,' he said to the prisoner. 'What was his name?'

The prisoner said nothing and Olumba hit him hard on the face.

'These men are tough thieves,' said one of Olumba's men.

'We're not thieves,' the prisoner said quietly.

Olumba became angry. 'Who is this rude, stupid man?' he asked.

'If you want to know my name, I am Wago the Leopard-killer,'[5] the prisoner replied.

Immediately there was silence. Everyone knew about Wago the Leopard-killer. Everyone knew that he was very brave and very strong. He was one of the bravest men in Aliakoro. He had killed three leopards and no other man had killed so many. Wago was an expert at hunting. No one knew how he caught his animals. He was tall, with muscles like elastic and he was a good wrestler.

Olumba respected[5] brave men. When he knew that his prisoner was Wago, he stopped being angry.

'But, Wago,' Olumba asked, 'why have you joined these thieves?'

'We're not thieves,' Wago replied. 'These fish are ours, so we cannot steal them.'

'Does the Pond of Wagaba belong to Aliakoro?' Olumba asked.

'Yes, it does,' replied Wago.

When Wago said this, Olumba and his men became so angry that they could not speak. Their raft floated along the ponds in silence. Quite suddenly, Wago pushed Olumba off the raft into the water. Wago dived off and disappeared. The night was very dark and nobody could see him.

Olumba climbed back onto the raft.

'Wago was tied up, wasn't he?' asked Ikechi.

'Of course he was,' replied Olumba angrily. 'I don't know how he got away.'

Olumba felt very angry with himself because Wago had escaped.

The two other prisoners were tied even more tightly so that they could not escape. At the edge of the ponds, they got off the rafts and Olumba's men followed their prisoners very carefully until they reached the village of Chiolu. They had brought back two prisoners from Aliakoro and the Chief, Eze Diali, would be pleased.

THREE

THE PRISONERS ARE SOLD
BACK TO ALIAKORO

In the morning, Eze Diali, the Chief of Chiolu, went to look at the two prisoners from Aliakoro.

'What are your names?' Eze Diali asked them.

The two prisoners told him their names and Diali smiled. He knew their fathers well.

Just then, three young men from the village of Aliakoro ran into the compound and greeted the Chief.

'What do you want?' he asked.

'We've come to take those two prisoners away,' said one of the three men. And he pointed at the two prisoners.

'That's not possible,' replied Diali. 'Your Chief, Eze Okehi, must come himself.'

'But we bring you a message from him,' one of them said.

'What is his message?' asked Eze Diali.

'Eze Okehi says you must first let the men go free. Then later you can both talk about the money you want for them.'

Chief Diali laughed when the man said this. He told the messengers to go back to Eze Okehi. They must tell him to come himself to Chiolu with his elders. Then they could talk about the problems of the poaching from the ponds.

Eze Diali was feeling very happy because his plan had been successful. Diali was a small man, but the people of Chiolu respected him very much. He was a good leader for the village.

A few hours later, the men arrived from Aliakoro. They were wearing war clothes. Eze Okehi, the Chief, walked in front. He was an older man than Eze Diali, although he was still very strong.

Eze Diali stood up to greet his visitors. He walked to meet Eze Okehi. He raised his right hand high above his head in greeting. Eze Okehi raised his right hand, too, and both men shook hands above their heads.

Kola nuts[3] were passed round until the bowl was nearly empty. Then Diali threw the nuts that were left in the bowl on to the ground. He offered then to Amadioha, the god of thunder and of the skies, and to Ogbunabali, the god who kills by night.

Eze Okehi stood up and began to speak,

'Men of Aliakoro, Leopard-killers, Eyes of the Night, I greet you!'

All the men shouted back with a roar.

'Men of Chiolu, who use fish for firewood, Terrors of the Forests, Hunters with Invisible Footprints, I greet you!'

There was another loud roar as the men of Chiolu accepted the greetings from Eze Okehi.

Eze Okehi went on talking. 'Eze Diali,' he said, 'we have come here to ask you to free the two young men you captured last night. We come to you as friends and we hope we can return to Aliakoro with our two men.'

'Your two men,' answered Eze Diali, 'were stealing fish from our pond – the Pond of Wagaba. When you have paid the money to get them back, you can take them with you.

'You say the Pond of Wagaba belongs to Aliakoro,' continued Eze Diali, 'but this pond has belonged to Chiolu for over thirty years. It belongs to us. If you want your two men, you must pay for them.'

'How much do you want?' asked Eze Okehi.

'We want eight hundred manillas,'[3] said Diali.

'What!' exclaimed Okehi, in surprise. 'Eight hundred manillas is too much to pay. We will pay you only two hundred manillas.'

'No. We want eight hundred,' repeated Diali. 'If you won't pay eight hundred manillas, you can't have the two men.'

'Eight hundred is too much,' repeated Okehi. 'Take five hundred.'

Eze Diali was going to agree when Olumba jumped forward to speak.

'The men of Aliakoro must say that the Pond of Wagaba belongs to Chiolu. Then, perhaps, we will take only five hundred manillas. But they must stop saying that the Pond belongs to them.'

'We will not say that,' a loud voice shouted from the men of Aliakoro.

Everyone looked round to see who was shouting. It was Wago, the Leopard-killer.

'Our fathers told us the Pond of Wagaba belongs to us,' said Wago. 'We will not let you keep it.'

Olumba walked nearer Wago. He was shaking with anger.

'My Lord, Eze Diali,' said Olumba, 'we will not take five hundred manillas. I led the men who captured these two prisoners. This man here, called Wago, was one of the poachers. I caught him, but he escaped from the raft. I heard him talking to his friends. He said that Eze Okehi has been telling his people for a long time that the Pond of Wagaba belongs to Aliakoro.'

Wago, the Leopard-killer, jumped forward.

'I swear by Ogbunabali,[2] the god of the night, that if anyone pays eight hundred manillas, I will cut off his head immediately,' he shouted.

There was silence and the men from both villages put their hands on their matchets. They were all waiting for Olumba and Wago to start fighting.

'Listen, everybody,' said Eze Diali, in a quiet voice. 'Take your hands away from your matchets. We are here to agree peacefully. If we don't agree today, then perhaps we can have another meeting later.'

Eze Diali went on talking quietly and the men became calm.

'It seems that the men from Aliakoro do not have eight hundred manillas with them,' he said. 'I think we should . . .'

Both sides started talking again.

In the end, Aliakoro paid six hundred manillas for the two prisoners.

'Now that is finished,' said Eze Okehi, 'I want to tell you this. We still say that the Pond of Wagaba belongs to Aliakoro. Perhaps we can share the pond.'

'Never! We shall never share it in my lifetime,' exclaimed Diali.

'Well, my men will fish there in my lifetime,' replied Okehi and he turned and walked away.

The men from Aliakoro left Chiolu immediately. They walked quietly through the village. Not one of them said good-bye.

FOUR

ELENDU JOINS THE FIGHT

About ten days later, Ikechi went to the Great Ponds to look at his fish-traps. Some of the traps were full of fish. He was very happy and he stayed at the Ponds until the sun went down. Then he decided to go home to Chiolu.

When he was leaving, he heard voices in the trees on the other side of the Pond. He looked through the trees and he saw several men. All of these men had matchets and bows and arrows. He guessed there were about twenty men altogether.

One of the men was Wago, the Leopard-killer. When Ikechi saw Wago his heart jumped[4] for, secretly, he was afraid of Wago.

Quietly, Ikechi moved away from Wago's men and ran to Chiolu. Back in the village, Ikechi told Eze Diali and the elders what he had seen.

The ikoro[3] sounded. Everyone who heard it knew that the meeting was going to be important. It was, also, very short. The men decided to guard the Pond from the poachers of Aliakoro. Olumba was chosen to make the plans.

When the meeting was over, the men of the village went to their houses to get ready for the following day. They sharpened their knives; they cut the leaves off palm trees to make arrows; and they put new strings on their bows.

Everything was ready. Then the men made sacrifices[2] to their gods and asked them for their help in the battle. They took out from their bags the charms which would help them to fight well. Olumba had a special charm he wore on his arm. If anyone shot an arrow at him, this charm would turn the arrow away.

Before Olumba left his house in the morning, his wives

came to say good bye to him. They knelt down in front of him and wished him luck. They tried not to cry since they believed their tears would make their men weak. But Oda, Olumba's third and youngest wife, came in carrying their little son in their arms. She started to cry. Olumba was angry with her, but he patted his son on the head. He loved his only son very, very much. Then he walked out of the compound.

When Olumba came near the Ponds he divided his men into three groups. Two groups were large and the third group was small. The two large groups hid in the trees on either side of the path. The small group went on to the Pond itself with Olumba. When they reached the Pond of Wagaba, Olumba saw Wago walking about talking to his men.

The villagers of Aliakoro were fishing and talking. They were all very happy. A messenger who had been watching the paths to Chiolu went to talk to Wago. He told Wago that some men were coming from Chiolu. Wago's men stood round him. They were preparing for the battle.

Olumba and his small group stood still. After a short time, Wago and his men came towards the men of Chiolu. Olumba was surprised that there were so many men with Wago.

When Wago was close enough, Olumba and his men shot their arrows. Two men fell to the ground, but the others kept coming. Olumba's men shot some more arrows. These arrows hit three more of Wago's men.

Wago the Leopard-killer began to run towards Olumba. His men started running too. Olumba's men shot some more arrows and then they turned and began to run away from Wago. Olumba had chosen men in his small group who could run very quickly. Soon the men of Aliakoro were getting slower, but Wago was running like the wind.

Suddenly Olumba shouted. Immediately many arrows were shot by one of the two groups which Olumba had left by

the side of the path. Many of these arrows hit the men of Aliakoro, but no arrow hit Wago. He ran on and on.

Olumba shouted once more, and more arrows came out of the trees. Olumba's second group were shooting their arrows. The men of Aliakoro were very surprised when they saw these arrows and they stopped running. Olumba shouted a third time. The men of Chiolu came out of the trees. Fierce fighting started. Olumba's men killed many of the men from Aliakoro with their matchets.

Suddenly more attackers came running up to help the men of Aliakoro. Olumba fought like a madman. Slowly the men of Chiolu drove the attackers back. Olumba thought he was winning.

Then, more attackers arrived. Olumba knew that Chiolu was not fighting only the men from Aliakoro. Wago had asked other villages to help him fight Chiolu. Olumba's men could not keep fighting the large groups of warriors who were coming to join the battle. He ordered his men to turn and run back home.

Luckily, Olumba and his men knew the secret paths back to Chiolu. Slowly, one by one, his men ran off the main path into the trees at the side. One by one they disappeared from the attackers.

At last, the attackers stopped.

'Which way have they gone?' asked their leader. His name was Elendu. He was from a village called Isiali.

'All ways,' replied one man. He waved his arms round in a semicircle, to show where the men had gone.

'We can't follow them,' answered Elendu.

The men sat down to rest. Then they went back to join Wago. Wago had a big cut on his shoulder, but Olumba had not killed him.

'What shall we do?' asked Elendu.

'Let's go back home,' answered Wago.

'I want to go to Chiolu to finish the fight,' said Elendu. 'I've lost many men and I haven't even one prisoner. What will I tell my Chief when I get back to Isiali?'

'If we go to Chiolu,' said another man, 'we must go at night, when the villagers are asleep.'

'I agree with that,' said Wago. 'But I can't come with you tonight because my wound hurts me. I'll give you some men from Aliakoro who know the paths to Chiolu well. They will show you the way.'

Then Wago got up and limped home alone.

FIVE

THE WOMEN ARE STOLEN
FROM CHIOLU

Olumba reached Chiolu early in the evening. He was very tired. He was also unhappy that his men had lost the fight.

Oda, Olumba's youngest wife, was pleased to see him and she got a hot bath ready for him. She massaged[5] his tired body and then he felt better. He was hungry so he had a quick meal.

Olumba walked round the village to see if his friends were safe and well. He visited Ikechi's compound first. The young man was at home. An arrow had gone through his right ear. Apart from that he was not hurt.

Olumba then went to visit some more compounds. When he felt tired he went home. He decided to visit the other compounds the next morning. He went straight to his bedroom, locked his door and slept.

Oda, Olumba's young wife, went to her own house with her little son and locked the door. Oda was pregnant[5] so she slept in a room by herself. She went to sleep, but very quickly woke up. She did not know why she had woken up, but she thought she had heard a noise. Olumba's dog began to bark. Oda listened for a while and then went to sleep again.

A loud bang woke her up. She sat up in her bed and saw a wide hole in the wall where the door had been. Somebody had kicked the door down. Two men ran into her room. They put a piece of cloth into her mouth and they tied her hands together. Quickly the men carried her away from her hut.

When they reached the path, the men put her down on the ground and told her to walk. She walked along with the men until they passed the edge of the village. There she saw three

other women from Chiolu. They all walked in silence.

Soon they arrived at a path which led to Elendu's village of Isiali. Elendu stopped and spoke.

'Men of Aliakoro, we will leave you now,' he said. 'We will come to your village tomorrow to see your Chief, Eze Okehi. We will take these four women with us.'

The men of Aliakoro did not want Elendu to take the four women, but they had to agree. They were afraid that Elendu might attack them if they tried to stop him.

'Elendu, you are a liar and a bad man,' said one of the men of Aliakoro.

Elendu laughed. 'You don't think we will return to Isiali without anything, do you?' he said. 'We've lost many men. We didn't know men from Aliakoro were such bad fighters.

'We will come tomorrow to your village,' Elendu continued. 'We want more than these four women as a reward.'

Elendu and his men left for Isiali taking the four women with them. The men from Aliakoro left for home too.

They had gone a little way when they heard footsteps behind them.

'Somebody is following us,' said one man.

'Let's run,' said another man.

They started running and the men of Chiolu followed them. Suddenly an arrow hit a man from Aliakoro and he fell to the ground. His friends ran into the trees. Olumba picked up the wounded man and pulled the arrow out of the man's neck.

'Tell me where the women are,' said Olumba in an angry voice.

The prisoner said something quietly. Olumba hit the man's face to make him say more.

'The men from Isiali have taken the women,' he said.

'Where are the men from Isiali now?' asked Olumba.

'They have gone to their village.'

Olumba bit[4] his teeth together. He was too late. It was dark and Olumba did not know the paths to Isiali. They spent the night in the forest and at dawn Olumba's men looked everywhere for the attackers from Isiali, but they did not see anyone. Olumba saw only some blood on the ground. He and his men returned to Chiolu.

Olumba was miserable and unhappy. He loved Oda very much indeed. She was his favourite wife and she was important to him because she was going to have another baby.

SIX

ONE WOMAN EQUALS
ONE MAN

That morning everyone in Chiolu was unhappy. Several men from the village had been killed or injured in the battle in the forest. Now men from Isiali had captured and taken away four women.

When Olumba reached his compound, he stood near Oda's house. He looked at the hole in the wall where the door had been. Then he walked to the house of his first wife, whose name was Nyoma. He saw his only son there. The son of Oda, his captured wife. His son's name was Nchelem. Olumba looked at Nchelem for a long time. He loved him very much.

At last, Olumba spoke to his first wife.

'Nyoma, you are now my son's mother. Look after him,' he said.

Nyoma took the little boy in her arms and left the house.

Olumba walked to Eze Diali's house. Diali was sitting by the fire. Several of his wives and children were sitting with him.

Olumba and Diali greeted each other.

'What did you do last night?' asked Diali.

'We couldn't find the women,' Olumba replied. 'But we captured one man. He told us that the men from Isiali had taken away our women. The men from Isiali were helping Aliakoro fight us.'

'Isiali is a long way from here,' said Diali.

'It is,' replied Olumba. 'Did the men take any women from your compound?'

'My daughter, Chisa, is gone,' he said.

Olumba was unhappy to hear this. He immediately thought about Ikechi. He knew Ikechi loved Chisa. He wondered if Ikechi knew that Chisa had been captured.

Ikechi did know. He was lying on his bed awake. He had not slept at all and his eyes were red with tiredness.

The ikoro sounded and the men of Chiolu met in Diali's reception hall. They all agreed they ought to go and see Eze Okehi, the Chief of Aliakoro.

*   *   *

Three days later, Olumba and his men were sitting in Eze Okehi's hall. Eze Diali was not there. He was sick and had stayed in Chiolu. Another elder, called Chituru, spoke instead of Diali.

Kola nuts were passed round to eat. Then Chituru stood up.

'Eze Okehi,' said Chituru, 'we have come to Aliakoro to take back our women. We want the women you stole the other night from Chiolu.'

'Chituru, I shall not waste your time,' replied Eze Okehi. 'You took two of our men a few weeks ago and we had to buy them back. Now you can pay for your women. We want four times four hundred manillas for each woman.'

The men of Chiolu were very surprised when Okehi said this. Never before had women been taken away as prisoners and never before had they been bought back.

Chituru and his men talked together to decide what to do.

'Eze Okehi,' said Chituru after their talk, 'we have decided not to give you any money for our women. These women were stolen. They were not captured in war.'

Eze Okehi stood up to speak.

'If you want to leave your women here, please do so,' the Chief said. 'But you captured one of our men the other night. We want him back. If you give him to us, we will give you one woman.'

Chituru, Olumba and their men talked among themselves to decide what to do. At last, Olumba stood up to speak.

'Listen, men of Aliakoro,' said Olumba. 'One man is not equal to one woman. Our village thinks that one man is equal to four women. If you want your man, you must give us our four women in return.'

'We will never do that,' shouted a loud voice. It was Wago.

'Are you equal to your wife?' Olumba asked Wago.

Wago thought for a moment and then he spoke.

'Your women will have children. If your children don't have their mothers, they will die,' said Wago. 'A woman is very important. So you can see why one woman is equal to one man.'

This idea seemed sensible and most people agreed with Wago. Even the men from Chiolu agreed with him.

'If you are ready,' said Chituru, 'we will give you back your one man.'

'You will have to wait until tomorrow,' Wago replied. 'We are not ready to give you the women now.'

Suddenly Olumba started to laugh very loudly. Everyone was amazed.

'Chituru, my lord,' Olumba said, 'we have been wasting our time. I had forgotten that our women are not here. They are at Isiali.'

'That is not true,' shouted Wago. 'The women are here.'

'Then let us see them,' said Olumba.

'Let us see our man,' demanded Wago.

'Your man is not far away,' said Olumba. 'If you want him we can show you him in a moment.'

Wago was going to speak, but Eze Okehi stopped him and spoke instead.

'We have given you an answer,' he said. 'If you want one woman back, come for her tomorrow. Then, when you have some money, you can have your three other women.'

'We will exchange our women and your man tomorrow at a place between the two villages,' Chituru said.

'That is good,' answered Okehi.

The meeting ended and Chituru took his men back to Chiolu.

* * *

The next day, the men of Chiolu took the prisoner from Aliakoro to the place between the two villages. They waited and waited but nobody came. It became dark so they returned to Chiolu. Chituru went back again the next day, but still the men of Aliakoro did not come.

Eze Diali talked with the elders.

'Either the women are at Isiali,' he said, 'or Eze Okehi does not want to keep his promise.'

'Our women are at Isiali,' Chituru replied. 'The men of Aliakoro are unable to give them to us. All the four women are very beautiful.'

'Let us think about what to do,' said Olumba. 'Then let us meet again in two or three days' time. We must decide to do something and we must do it well. We must not make a mistake.'

SEVEN

THE CHIEF OF ALIAKORO
BECOMES AFRAID

Four days after the meeting with the men of Chiolu, Eze
Okehi sat resting in his house. It was a warm afternoon and
most of the women in Aliakoro had gone to work on the farms.

The children in the village were playing games. They
were running around after each other and climbing trees.
After a while, Okehi's son became bored and tired and went
to sit in his father's compound.

Suddenly he saw some birds hopping about picking up
insects and seeds to eat. The boy picked up some stones and
threw them at the birds. Most of the birds flew away, but two
birds did not move.

Okehi's son threw two more stones at these birds, but they
still did not fly away.

The boy became interested so he tiptoed towards the two
birds. Okehi had seen his son throwing stones, but he did not
take much notice of him.

The boy moved nearer and nearer the birds and still they
did not fly away. They just hopped about and were not afraid
of him. When he was near enough, he jumped forward and
caught one of them in his hands. The other bird hopped a few
feet away and then stopped. The boy went after this bird and
caught it also. Then he ran to his father waving the two birds
in the air and shouting excitedly.

Eze Okehi was amazed when he saw his son with the two
birds in his hands.

'Did you hit them with stones?' he asked his son.

'No, father.'

'Have you hurt them?'

'No, father.'

'Bring them here,' said Okehi. He looked carefully at the birds. They were strong and healthy.

The two birds stayed in the boy's hands singing happily.

Okehi looked unhappy. He was very frightened. These birds would bring him bad luck in the future.

'Let them go. Let them fly away,' Okehi told his son.

The boy stood there, first looking at the birds and then at his father. Why was his father telling him to let the birds fly away?

'Let them fly away,' Okehi said again, more firmly.

The boy threw the two birds into the air and they flew away still singing.

Okehi was very, very worried. He went to his bedroom and sat quietly. He wanted to think about what he had seen. He wondered why the birds had let themselves be caught by his little son.

By evening time, Okehi was so unhappy that he went to visit his friend, Igwu, the dibia. A dibia is a man who has power to talk to the gods. He can look into the past and can say what will happen in the future. Igwu used drums to talk to the gods and to help him tell the future.

Okehi gave Igwu two manillas and Igwu began to beat his drums. He beat them hard and he began to sweat. His eyes shone with brightness.

'Two birds,' Igwu shouted out at last.

Okehi was very surprised. He had not said anything to Igwu about his son and the two birds. Okehi had often seen Igwu's magic, but Okehi was still surprised.

'You have come to see me about two birds,' Igwu said again.

He stopped drumming for a few seconds.

'Yes, dibia,' replied Okehi.

Igwu started drumming again.

'Your son caught two birds while he was playing.'

'That's true,' answered Okehi.

'He did not use a knife.'

'That's true,' Okehi said again.

'He didn't even throw a stone.'

'That's true.'

'Ali, the god of the earth, is very angry,' Igwu said.

'Why is Ali angry?' asked Okehi.

'The women you took from Chiolu must be returned,' answered Igwu. 'One of them is pregnant and the god of the earth does not allow anyone to harm any woman with a child.'

'But men from Isiali stole the four women,' replied Okehi. 'Not men from Aliakoro.'

'Yes,' answered Igwu, 'but you asked the men from Isiali to help you fight Chiolu.'

'What must I do now?' asked Okehi.

Igwu started drumming again.

'You must do two things,' answered Igwu. 'First you must make a sacrifice to please Ali, the god of the earth. Then you must return the women to Chiolu. Then Ali will forgive you.'

'Must I return all the four women?' Okehi asked in a worried voice.

'You must return the woman who is pregnant,' said Igwu. 'You must return her to her family.'

The next day, Eze Okehi made a sacrifice. Then he sent Wago with some men to Isiali to fetch the four women who had been taken from Chiolu. The Chief of Isiali refused to hand over the women. He wanted a lot of money in exchange for them.

The next day, Wago and his men went to Isiali with the money. The men in Isiali took the money from Wago, but they had only two of the women with them. Unfortunately, Oda and Chisa were not in Isiali.

'Where are the other two women?' asked Wago.

'We have sold them,' replied Elendu.

'Who to?' asked Wago.

'I don't know. Some men came here and asked for some female slaves.[3] We sold the two most beautiful women to them.'

When Wago heard this news, he was both disappointed and afraid. He did not know what to do. But he took the two other women home to Okehi.

When Wago told Okehi that Olumba's wife and Diali's daughter had been sold as slaves, Okehi was horrified and very miserable.

Eze Okehi then went to see Igwu, the dibia, again. Igwu

told him to make another sacrifice to please the god, Ali, until Oda was found. It was very important because Oda was pregnant.

Meanwhile messengers went to Chiolu from Okehi. They met Eze Diali and agreed upon a date for the exchange of the two women from Chiolu and the prisoner from Aliakoro.

EIGHT

THE WAR BEGINS

Four days later, the warriors from Aliakoro went to the meeting place between the two villages to meet the men from Chiolu.

Wago, the Leopard-killer, was worried when he did not see Olumba at the meeting. He thought immediately that Olumba must be hiding somewhere and waiting to attack them at any time.

The old men from Chiolu sat quietly on logs of trees. They were not worried. Both sides greeted each other and then Eze Okehi spoke.

'We have brought two women with us,' he said. 'The other two women you can have later on. If you bring your prisoner, we can make the exchange now.'

The drums sounded and the man and one of the two women was exchanged.

'There is one women left,' continued Okehi. 'Do you want to pay the money for her now or later?'

In the end, Diali paid four times four hundred manillas for the second woman. The drums sounded and everyone got up to leave to go home to their villages.

Wago was still very worried. He wondered why Olumba had not been at the exchange of the prisoners. One of the women might have been Olumba's wife, Oda.

Wago and his men started to go back through the forest to Aliakoro. When they came near their village, a warrior from Aliakoro ran towards them.

'Have you seen Okasi?' he asked, panting. He was out of breath.

'Where is he?' asked Wago.

'We sent him to you.'

'Why?'

'To ask for help,' the warrior replied. 'Men from Chiolu attacked the village after you had left for the meeting.'

The men rushed back to the village and ran to their compounds. They looked everywhere to find people who were missing. Soon everyone met in Okehi's reception hall. They were all very miserable. Three women were missing. One of them was one of Okehi's wives and another was the daughter of Wago. She was only twelve years old.

A search party was sent out and they found the dead body of Okasi on the path to Chiolu. A very big arrow had gone deep into his stomach.

*　　　*　　　*

Everyone in Aliakoro was very frightened and unhappy. Eze Okehi had a pain in his back, but he still went to meetings. The villagers all agreed that they had to fight the people of Chiolu.

Eze Okehi became more and more worried. Ali, the god of the earth, had told him to give back the pregnant woman to Chiolu. He had not done this yet. He did not know how to find her. Okehi made more sacrifices to please Ali. Slowly Okehi became ill with worry and fear. Most of the time he stayed in his bed.

As Eze Okehi became less powerful in the village, Wago became more important. He was still very angry because his daughter had been stolen and he wanted another big fight with Chiolu.

But Wago knew that if Aliakoro fought Chiolu, Aliakoro would lose. He therefore decided to make the people of Chiolu too frightened to walk about their village. He wanted to make it unsafe for anyone in the village to walk about at any time of the day or night.

Wago sent men to stand on the paths to Chiolu. He told them they must kill or capture any villager walking about Chiolu. Men from Aliakoro surrounded the village at night. They were ready to kill anyone they saw.

One night the men of Aliakoro attacked an old woman and her children in Chiolu. The men from Chiolu caught the attackers and killed two of them. Then they took the two dead bodies and put them outside Okehi's door. When the Chief saw them, he was very frightened.

Even Wago was horrified that two men from Aliakoro had been killed so cruelly. One of the two men had had his head chopped off. Wago and the people became very angry. They were so angry they decided to kill as many people in Chiolu as they could. Each village now really hated the people of the other.

Everyone in both villages was frightened. Nobody went to work on their farms. The women dared not to go to the stream for water.

The fighting became so bad that the other villages in the Erekwi clan also suffered. The Chiefs of these other villages met to decide what to do. They met in Isiali, which was the oldest village in the area. They decided to have a meeting of all the villages in the Erekwi clan and they asked the men of Aliakoro and of Chiolu to the meeting.

NINE

OLUMBA TAKES THE OATH

The meeting of the Chiefs of all the villages in the Erekwi clan took place in Isiali. The women in Isiali cooked lots of food for all the important people who were there. The Chiefs wore their special clothes. These clothes were very beautiful and expensive. Nobody in the village had ever seen such beautiful clothes before.

After the midday meal, the meeting began. The Chiefs went into a separate room to talk and to try to find the answer to the problem of the Pond of Wagaba.

'Let us divide the pond between them,' said one man.

'Let them fish in the pond in different years,' said another.

None of them could find a good answer.

'We can do only one thing,' said another Chief. 'We must let the gods decide. One man must swear by the name of a god[2] that the Pond of Wagaba belongs to his village.'

The next day the Chiefs told the people what they had decided.

Everyone accepted their decision.

Then Olumba spoke.

'I will swear for Chiolu,' he said. 'Tell me the name of the god I must swear by. The Pond of Wagaba is ours. I know the gods will help us.'

When he said this, everyone stopped talking.

'Which god do you want Olumba to swear by?' one of the Chiefs asked Okehi.

'We choose the god Ogbunabali, the god of the night,' Okehi answered.

People began to whisper to each other. Ogbunabali was one of the most powerful gods in the Erekwi clan. He always killed at night. Most villages had shrines[2] for this god, but the biggest shrine was at Isiali.

Olumba sat still. He did not move at all. His strong arms were folded across his chest and he bit his teeth together.

After a few seconds, Olumba stood up.

'I agree to swear by Ogbunabali, for Chiolu,' he said.

Early the next morning the Chiefs and their elders went to the shrine of Ogbunabali at Isiali. Olumba stood in front of the shrine. He wore no clothes, but only a piece of cloth around his stomach. In a solemn voice he repeated the words after the priest.[2]

'I swear by Ogbunabali the god of the night that the Pond of Wagaba belongs to Chiolu.

If this is not true, let me die within six months;

If true, let me live.'

The priest waved the image[2] of Ogbunabali round Olumba's head three times and the swearing was over. If Olumba died within six months, the pond belonged to Aliakoro. If he lived for six months, then it truly belonged to Chiolu.

Then Eze Diali spoke.

'Before we leave this shrine, the Chief of Aliakoro must promise us that his men will not try to harm Olumba. They must not hurt his body or attack his spirit.'[2]

'That is right,' said the priest. Then he held a horn full of wine and poured it on to the ground. As he did this he said:

'Those who would harm Olumba
By the knife or the barbed arrow,
By strange charms or witchcraft,
Kill them Ogbunabali, King of the Night,
Kill them and show signs.'

Olumba left the shrine feeling a different person. He had never felt like it before. He seemed to be in a dream. He

walked back to Chiolu slowly. He hardly said anything to his friends. The walk made him feel better and his thoughts became clearer as he got nearer his village.

When he reached his compound, Olumba told his first wife, Nyoma, what had happened. She began to cry when he told her that he had sworn on the god Ogbunabali. She was afraid because Ogbunabali was such a powerful god.

* * *

The next day, Eze Diali held a meeting of the elders and the most important warriors.

'This meeting is about Olumba,' Diali said. 'Olumba now belongs to all of us and we have to keep him safe. What shall we do to keep him from harming himself?'

'He must not travel,' said one man.

'He must not climb trees,' said another.

'He must eat only the food that his first wife cooks.'

'He must not go to his farm.'

Everybody suggested other things that Olumba must not do.

'You have heard what the elders have said,' Diali said to Olumba. 'Let me tell you again so that you won't forget.

'First, you must not travel out of the village. You must eat only the food your wife cooks. And you must not climb any trees.'

Olumba listened carefully. Everyone was looking at him. At last, he spoke.

'Elders and people,' he said. 'I'm sure everything you've said is good for me. But I have two things to say to you.'

'Tell us, please,' said the Chief.

'Firstly, I must look after my palm trees and take the wine from them. So I shall have to climb trees. Secondly, I must work on my farm which is a long way from the village.'

The elders talked among themselves for some time. Then Chituru spoke.

'Ikechi, come here please,' he said. 'Ikechi, you will collect the wine from Olumba's palm-wine trees for him.'

'I will do that,' Ikechi replied.

'Olumba,' said Chituru, 'the people in the village will do the work on your farm.'

Olumba laughed.

'You will make me like a woman,' he said.

'It won't be for long,' replied Chituru. 'Six months will go by very quickly. But you must not be afraid.'

'The gods are wise,' said Diali. 'I am sure Ogbunabali will take good care of you.'

TEN

OLUMBA BECOMES CARELESS

One month had gone by and Olumba was still safe and well. He was not so afraid now, but he was bored because the elders did not let him do any work. He could not hunt, collect his palm wine, or go to the farm. He could only walk from one end of the village to the other.

One evening, Ikechi came to collect the palm wine from two trees in Olumba's compound.

Both men went to look at the palm trees.

'Look at that,' said Ikechi. He pointed to the top of one of the palm-wine trees.

'What is it?' asked Olumba.

'It's a nest of wasps.'

'Do you know what to do with it?'

'No, I don't.'

'Then I'll help you,' said Olumba.

'No. You mustn't. Remember, Olumba, that you must not climb trees. Let me get the nest down.'

'Now, don't be worried, Ikechi. I've never fallen from a tree. I won't die if I climb the tree once only.'

'I don't think you ought to climb,' Ikechi replied.

'I'll show you tomorrow, anyway,' smiled Olumba.

So the following morning Olumba and Ikechi went back to the tree. Ikechi threw a large stone at the nest of wasps, but he did not hit it. He tried a second time and missed again.

'Wait a moment and I'll show you,' said Olumba.

Olumba went back home and brought back a long ladder. He put the ladder against the tree and climbed it. He carried his matchet in his hand.

'Watch what I do,' he told Ikechi.

Suddenly a bird flew past the nest and frightened the wasps. The wasps flew out of the nest and attacked Olumba. Hundreds of wasps were stinging Olumba's face. He cried out in pain. He waved his matchet about to keep the wasps away, but they still attacked and stung him.

Olumba held the ladder with one hand and tried to cover his face with the other hand. He began to climb down the ladder two steps at a time. When he was half-way down, he slipped and fell. He crashed to the ground. He lay there, breathing loudly. Blood was coming out of his nose.

Ikechi ran towards Olumba. He screamed loudly in fright. He screamed again and again and people in other compounds heard him.

Many neighbours rushed to the place and they were afraid

when they saw Olumba on the ground. They stood there for a while and looked at him. Finally, some of them carried Olumba into the nearest house. Olumba was alive, but he was unconscious.[5]

When the news spread through the village, Eze Diali went to see Olumba.

'What happened?' Diali asked Ikechi.

'Olumba climbed a palm-wine tree to get down a nest of wasps at the top. I told him not to, but he said he would be all right.'

'And the wasps stung him?' asked Diali.

'Yes. Hundreds of them attacked him.'

Diali looked closely at Olumba. Then he spoke to Chituru.

'There is only one dibia who can make Olumba better. His name is Anwuanwu and he lives in Abii.'

So twenty strong men took Olumba on a light wooden bed to Abii. They covered him with wrappers.[3] Olumba moved a few times on his bed. The carriers were happy because they knew that he was still alive.

After a long journey, they reached Anwuanwu's house at about midnight. The men knocked at the door.

'Come in,' answered the dibia.

'Anwuanwu, we are in great trouble,' said Ikechi.

'Bring Olumba inside the house,' answered Anwuanwu. 'I knew you were coming.'

The men took Olumba inside and placed the bed gently on the ground. The dibia started to throw his cowries[2] around on the floor. The cowries would tell him what to do.

At last, Anwuanwu spoke. 'The god Ogbunabali has not hurt Olumba. But ordinary men are hurting him,' the dibia said.

'Which men?' asked Ikechi.

'I shall tell you later. We must now try to keep Olumba from dying.'

43

ELEVEN

ENEMIES AT WORK

The dibia ordered the men to place some logs on the ground and to put Olumba's bed on top of them. Then he massaged Olumba's body. He noticed that Olumba had fallen on his back.

Anwuanwu made a small fire under Olumba's bed. He threw different plants into the fire. The fire became hotter and hotter, and the heat made Olumba feel very uncomfortable.

The dibia started to massage Olumba again. Then Olumba opened his eyes and spoke.

'Where am I?' Olumba asked in a quiet voice.

'You fell from a palm-wine tree. Soon you will feel better.'

Anwuanwu continued to massage Olumba's body. Slowly the injured man closed his eyes again and went into a quiet sleep.

'Now tell us,' said Ikechi, 'which men are harming Olumba.'

'Men are at work,' said the dibia.

'Which men?' Ikechi asked again.

Anwuanwu poured some powder into his left hand. He rubbed some of the powder over his eyes. His eyes filled with tears. He went outside and blew the rest of the powder into the air. Then he hurried inside again.

'Now we shall see who is more powerful,' the dibia said.

Anwuanwu began to laugh and behave in the most unusual way. The men from Chiolu did not understand what he was trying to do.

'Your enemies made Olumba fall from that tree,' the dibia said at last. 'They have used a powerful dibia. This dibia is harming Olumba's mind so that he will do careless things.'

'But the priest of Ogbunabali said that any men who tried to harm Olumba would die,' answered Ikechi.

'That may be true, but wicked dibias can do many things.'

'Can a dibia be more powerful than a god?' asked Ikechi.

'Yes, sometimes,' Anwuanwu replied. 'If the Pond of Wagaba really belongs to Aliakoro, Ogbunabali will not harm the men there. He will harm Olumba.'

'But what happens if the Pond truly belongs to Chiolu?'

'The god will be just and fair,' said Anwuanwu. 'Ogbunabali is a powerful god. No good dibia will try to fight him.'

'What shall we do now?' asked Ikechi.

'Your elders must decide what to do. If they want me to help, please let me know. At the moment I will help Olumba get better,' answered Anwuanwu.

Ikechi stayed to look after Olumba, but the other men went back to Chiolu.

When they arrived back, they told Olumba's wives that their husband was safe and would get better.

*   *   *

Five days after Olumba's fall from the tree, three men walked into Eze Diali's reception hall. They were from Aliakoro.

'My Lord,' one of the men said. 'We bring important messages from our Chief, Eze Okehi.'

'Sit down, my son,' Diali answered politely.

Diali called the elders to come and see him. Kola nuts were passed around to welcome the messengers.

'Now, what do you want to tell us?' asked Diali.

'I am Wago the Leopard-killer,' said Wago looking carefully at Diali.

'What news have you come to tell us?' asked Diali.

'Eze Okehi has heard that Olumba is dead. Therefore the Pond of Wagaba now belongs to Aliakoro,' Wago said.

Eze Diali laughed quietly.

'You seem to know more about life in Chiolu than we do,' he said. 'Olumba is not dead.'

'He is,' answered Wago. 'Our men have not seen him for a long time and we have been watching Chiolu very carefully. Olumba must be dead. Where is he?'

'We cannot tell you,' answered Diali.

'Because he is dead,' said Wago.

'Go back to Aliakoro and tell your Chief that Olumba is alive. If he doesn't believe me, then the elders can come and see Olumba.'

Diali looked at Wago and continued talking.

'Tell them to come in eight days' time,' he said.

After Wago and his men had left, Diali and his elders laughed and laughed at Wago's mistake. They laughed more than they had done for a long, long time.

After eight days, Eze Okehi himself went to Chiolu. He was ill, but he wanted to be sure that Olumba was dead and that the Pond of Wagaba belonged to Aliakoro.

The men from Aliakoro argued for a long time with Diali. They kept on saying that Olumba was dead.

Then suddenly Olumba walked into the reception hall. He stood there looking at Eze Okehi. Okehi could not believe it.

Eze Okehi was very disappointed because he had asked Igwu, the dibia, to make Olumba behave carelessly. He knew that Olumba had climbed the palm tree and had fallen.

But Igwu's powers were not strong enough. Olumba was still alive. The dibia would have to try harder the next time.

TWELVE

IGWU COOKS OLUMBA

Later the next day, the important elders of Aliakoro met in Igwu's house. Igwu told them what he wanted.

'I shall need a small piece of Olumba's clothing or anything that he has touched,' said Igwu. 'How can we get this? It is very important for me.'

'That will be difficult,' said Okehi. 'But we must do it.'

No one spoke.

At last, Wago answered.

'I'll get a piece of Olumba's clothing or anything else you want,' he said.

In the evening, Wago went to Chiolu. He walked along the quiet paths and not along the main one. He arrived at Chiolu when it was dark.

Wago had a simple plan. He was going to hide near the place where Olumba took his bath. There was a fence round the bath place and Olumba always hung his wrapper over the fence.

For two days Wago was unlucky because Olumba took his bath in the daytime. During the day Wago hid himself and nobody saw him.

On the third day, Olumba took his bath after dark. He hung his wrapper over the fence and Wago cut off a small piece from the corner. Olumba did not hear anything and Wago ran back happily to Aliakoro.

The next day, Igwu the dibia began his work against Olumba. He had never done anything as bad as he was going to do now.

He boiled a large pot of water. He threw the piece of Olumba's wrapper into the boiling water and then other things he had collected. He then threw in the skin of a snake. And finally he put a piece of wood into the pot. Igwu had cut this piece of wood so that it looked like Olumba's body. Before he threw this piece of wood into the pot, Igwu called out Olumba's name three times.

When the mixture was boiling, Igwu took a long, thin knife. He put the point of the knife through Olumba's face and then into his stomach.

Igwu had finished his work. The piece of wood in the pot would cook. Igwu was trying to cook Olumba.

The next day, when Olumba was sitting with his wife, Wogari, he noticed that a small piece of his wrapper was missing.

'I wonder when this was torn off,' he said to Wogari.

'What, my husband?'

'One corner of my wrapper has been torn off,' Olumba replied.

'The rats must have eaten it,' she said. 'I must fill the holes up in your bedroom walls so the rats cannot get in.'

'Yes, you must, or I shall have no wrappers left,' laughed Olumba.

Olumba sat thinking. There were three months left. If he was not dead after three more months, the Pond of Wagaba would belong to Chiolu for ever. If Ogbunabali was going to kill him, Olumba wondered why he was waiting so long.

Then Olumba heard a voice in his head. It got louder and louder.

'The god may kill you on the last day of the six months,' the voice said.

Olumba had heard this voice many times before. He had even started giving answers to it.

'No,' said Olumba to himself. 'The god will not kill me on the last day.'

At midnight, when he was in bed, Olumba woke up suddenly. He was sweating and his body was trembling. He got out of bed and went into Wogari's bedroom and lay beside her.

'Wogari, I don't feel well,' Olumba said quietly.

'What's the matter?'

'I don't know.'

'Shall I light the lamp?' asked Wogari.

'Yes,' replied Olumba.

Wogari lit the oil lamp and looked at her husband. His eyes were shut and his breathing was loud. Sweat was running down his body like little rivers. A great heat came from him, as if he were on fire.

Wogari called Nyoma, Olumba's other wife. Nyoma ran off quickly to find Eze Diali.

Diali came and looked at Olumba for a few moments. He immediately sent Ikechi to find the dibia, Anwuanwu, who had helped Olumba before. He was the best dibia for miles and miles around.

It was a long night. Olumba became worse and worse, but he did not die. In the morning, Anwuanwu arrived in Chiolu.

He went into Olumba's room and looked at him. Then he laughed out loud. The elders watched him and did not understand why he was laughing. Then he took out his cowries and threw them around on the floor. He laughed again.

'I thought so,' he said at last. 'Olumba is being cooked.'

'Who is cooking Olumba?' asked the elders.

'Your enemies in Aliakoro,' replied the dibia.

Then Anwuanwu spoke to Olumba.

'Have you been hearing voices?' he asked.

'Yes,' the sick man said quietly.

'Are any of your wrappers missing?'

'No, but the rats have eaten the corner off one of them.'

Anwuanwu looked at Olumba's wrapper and smiled.

'A rat has not done this,' the dibia said. 'The piece has been cut off with a sharp knife.'

'Do you mean that somebody came here from Aliakoro and cut a piece off Olumba's wrapper?' Diali asked. He could not believe what the dibia was saying.

'Yes.'

'But what did he want the piece of cloth for?'

'To put in the cooking pot,' Anwuanwu answered.

Diali seemed less frightened when he understood what was happening.

'So the god Ogbunabali is not harming Olumba,' he said.

'No,' replied Anwuanwu. 'It is a dibia in Aliakoro.'

'Can you save Olumba for us?'

'Yes, I can,' Anwuanwu answered with a smile.

Anwuanwu spent two busy days doing things to stop Olumba from dying. Slowly Olumba got better.

After another four days, Anwuanwu was ready to leave Chiolu. Diali paid him a lot of money for saving Olumba.

'We would like your help for the next three months,' he said. 'You are the only person who can help us.'

'I will work for you for as long as you like,' answered the dibia. 'But I don't have to stay in Chiolu. I can work from my own village.'

Anwuanwu then said good-bye and returned to his village. He left many charms with Olumba. These charms would help him fight the dibia in Aliakoro.

THIRTEEN

THE SEARCH FOR
THE WOMEN

Although Olumba was still alive, his body was getting weaker and weaker. He did not seem to care about life any more. He was quiet and did not speak much. He ate very little food. He was often angry with his wives for no reason. He spent most of his time holding his little son, Nchelem, in his arms.

Eze Diali knew that there was only one way to make Olumba happy again. He had to find Oda, Olumba's lost wife, the mother of Nchelem.

The Chief decided to send out a search party to look for Oda, and Chisa, his own daughter. The search party would probably not find the two women, but Olumba would be happier.

Diali chose Ikechi as one of the four men in the search party. He spoke to Ikechi before the men left the Chief's house.

'Do your best, my son,' said Diali. 'You know how important these two women are to this village. If you can find Oda, we might keep the Pond of Wagaba for ever because Olumba will become strong again. And you know how important my daughter, Chisa, is to me. I know you love her too.'

A lump came into Ikechi's throat[4] when he heard Chisa's name. He said good-bye to Diali. Then he went to Olumba's compound. Olumba was sitting in his reception hall. He was holding Nchelem in his arms.

'Olumba, we are leaving now,' said Ikechi.

'Do your best,' Olumba replied briefly.

A few days later, Ikechi and his three friends crept quietly

back into the village. They had failed to find the two women and they did not want anyone to see them. All four men looked very sad.

Ikechi went to tell Eze Diali about the journey.

'We went first to Isiali and stayed there for one night,' he said. 'We spoke to Elendu. He said he had sold the two women to some men who had come from the other side of the river. He did not know who these men were or where they came from.'

Eze Diali listened quietly. He felt sad. Ikechi went on with his story.

'We then went to a village by the river. We found out that two men and two women had been seen there some months before. The men were taking the two women to the other side of the river, but their boat turned over in the water. The villagers thought that all the four people had been drowned.'

Tears were in Ikechi's eyes as he spoke.

Diali still said nothing so Ikechi continued.

'We went to the village across the river and spoke to the Chief. He told us that no women had arrived in the village. He knew nothing about the two women. So we came back here.'

'Thank you,' said Diali. 'I think you've done all you could. As soon as the six months of Olumba's oath is at an end, we will send another search party.

'Be careful what you tell Olumba,' Diali went on. 'Don't tell him that Oda and Chisa are probably drowned in the river. Say they are still missing.'

Ikechi left Diali with tears in his eyes. He thought about the last few months. He had become a man, but he hated the war now. He wished that the Pond of Wagaba had never belonged to Chiolu. He thought of Chisa. What a wonderful wife she would have made!

Suddenly Ikechi felt older and more thoughtful. Now he was a harder and a wiser person. He knew that sadness comes into everyone's life.

Thinking these thoughts, Ikechi went off to tell Olumba about his journey.

FOURTEEN

THE SICKNESS SPREADS
IN CHIOLU

When Olumba heard Ikechi's story, he wanted to go himself to find his wife, Oda. Two things stopped him. The first was that his son, Nchelem, was ill and would miss him if he went.

Secondly, Nyoma, his wife, was also ill. Nyoma had a very bad cough and a pain in her chest. The local dibia gave her some medicine, but Nyoma got weaker and thinner every day.

After a few days, she was as thin as a broomstick.

Olumba became weaker too. He now looked like a very old man. Everyone thought he would die at any time. Olumba himself was sure that he was going to die. He called Eze Diali and some other friends to his reception hall.

'You can all see what is happening,' he said. 'My wife, Nyoma, is going to die. I shall probably die next. If my other wife, Wogari, and my daughters do not die too, please look after them.'

Diali and the others sat in silence. Suddenly Olumba got up from his seat and went outside the house. He stood there with his arms stretched up to the sky.

'Ogbunabali, god of the night, I am sure you are listening to me,' Olumba shouted. 'Save my wife, Nyoma. She did not swear to you. Only I swore. Let me die, but save my wife.'

Nyoma did not die that night. She felt a little better in the morning and she asked for some water and then for some food.

A few days later, Wogari, Olumba's other wife, began to cough too. She felt very ill. She did not want Olumba to know and so she pretended to be all right.

Eze Diali came to see how Nyoma was.

'She's a little better,' said Olumba.

'But how are you today?' Olumba asked the Chief. 'I heard yesterday that you were not well.'

'I am well, but I have a sore throat. When I swallow any food I feel a pain,' said Diali. 'Many people in the village seem to be ill. My little daughter, Ihunda, is sick. She has a cough like your wife and she has pains in her chest.'

That night, little Ihunda died.

That same night, a young man aged twenty died. Suddenly everyone became very frightened. So many people were dying so quickly.

The people of Chiolu met in Diali's reception hall. They decided that some of the elders should go to Aliakoro. They wanted to ask Okehi to release Olumba from his oath[2] to Ogbunabali. They agreed that Aliakoro could have the Pond of Wagaba if their families did not die.

Olumba got up to speak.

'Men of Chiolu. Listen to me,' he said. 'The image of the god was waved three times round my head. My two wives and my son are ill. But please do not go to Aliakoro. In twenty days' time my oath will be at an end. Can't we wait twenty more days? Remember – whoever gets the Pond of Wagaba will then keep it for ever.'

Everybody looked at Olumba. They did not know how he could speak such brave words.

Everyone started talking quietly. Suddenly a scream was heard. Somebody else had died.

'Eze Diali,' the people shouted. 'Do something or everyone in this village will soon be dead.'

Then they all quickly left the meeting and went home.

Olumba went back to his compound. He found Wogari lying on her bed. She was very, very ill. Olumba knew that Wogari was going to die soon. There was no need to go to find the dibia. It was too late.

In the middle of the night, another loud cry told the village that another person had died.

FIFTEEN

A SURPRISE FOR THE
ELDERS IN CHIOLU

Eze Diali lay sick in his bed. He had began to think that
Ogbunabali was slowly killing all the people of Chiolu in
the night.

Diali blamed himself because he had started the War of
the Great Ponds. He remembered the day he sent Olumba
and his friends to capture the poachers from the Pond of
Wagaba. Now life was very different. His plans and hopes for
the village had all gone wrong.

The elders wanted to go to Aliakoro to ask Eze Okehi to
release Olumba from his oath. In the end, Diali agreed and
six men went off to Aliakoro.

Wezume was now the most important elder who was not sick so he led the six men. They did not see anybody on the way to Aliakoro.

'Eze Okehi will be very happy,' one of the men said. 'The Pond of Wagaba will soon belong to him.'

They walked slowly through the village of Aliakoro.

'Someone is dead here,' said one man.

They looked at a new grave in one of the compounds.

'That's true.'

'And here is another new grave,' said Wezume.

Before they came to Okehi's compound, they saw four new graves.

When they came into Okehi's compound they found many people sitting there. It was easy to see that they were unhappy.

The men from Chiolu walked in carefully. No one took much notice of them.

At last, one of the elders of Aliakoro spoke.

'You are from Chiolu, aren't you?' he asked. 'I know your faces.'

'Yes. We come from Chiolu,' replied Ikechi.

'How is Olumba?'

'Olumba is well. Tell me. What is happening here?'

'One of Eze Okehi's children is very ill and will soon die.'

'What is the illness?'

'The people here call it wonjo.'

'Wonjo?' asked Ikechi.

'Yes. Five people have already died from it,' said one of the men of Aliakoro.

Wezume called his men to one side.

'I think it is the same disease as we have in Chiolu,' he said.

'I think so, too,' replied Ikechi.

'What shall we do?' asked Wezume.

No one spoke for a moment. They were too busy thinking

about the illness which was killing people in both Aliakoro and Chiolu.

They decided to ask to see Eze Okehi.

'Can we see Eze Okehi?' asked Wezume.

'Yes. He's in that room over there with his friends.'

When they saw the Chief, he seemed to be a very different man. He had changed a lot since they had last seen him. He was not really sick, but he looked much worse than a sick man.

'We are sorry that your child is so ill,' said Wezume.

'Thank you for your kind thoughts,' replied Okehi.

'Now we shall leave you,' said Wezume.

'Tell me what you've come for,' answered the Chief. 'Surely you haven't come all the way from Chiolu just to greet us?'

'That's true,' replied Wezume. 'We have a message for the whole village.'

'Is it an important message? If it is, then I'll call all the elders to come and hear it.'

Many of the elders came hurrying to the reception hall. Wago, the Leopard-killer, came too.

'What is your message?' Okehi asked as soon as the elders were seated.

Wezume did not speak for some time. He was trying to think of something to say.

'What do you want to tell us?' asked another voice. It was Wago who was asking the question.

'We have come with a message from Chiolu,' said Wezume after a long time.

'Say it then,' Wago said quickly.

'It is this. We know that many people in Aliakoro are sick and that many are dying,' said Wezume. 'The people of Chiolu are now ready to let you release Olumba from his oath. This will stop more of your people dying.'

The men of Aliakoro listened in silence. Wezume continued talking.

'In about twelve days' time, there will be a new moon and the six months' waiting will be over. We are sure that Olumba will live for the next twelve days. We only want to help you. Both Chiolu and Aliakoro belong to the same clan.'

The Chief, Okehi, stared at the visitors. He looked unhappy. The elders sat without moving.

Suddenly like a crash of thunder, Wago's voice broke the silence. He let out a loud, loud laugh. His shoulders shook and his head rolled from side to side as he laughed.

The elders of Aliakoro watched him. They were surprised at Wago's behaviour and they felt uncomfortable.

Wago stopped laughing as quickly as he had started. He looked at the visitors. Then he stood up to speak. He did not ask permission from Okehi to speak, but nobody stopped him.

'Do you think you are clever?' Wago roared. His eyes flashed.

'What do you mean?' Wezume asked quietly.

'Do you think you are clever?' Wago asked again. He started to laugh once more.

'Say what you want to say,' answered Wezume angrily. 'We are not children and you should not ask us childish questions.'

'Listen, men of Aliakoro,' said Wago. 'I have been watching Chiolu for the past sixteen days. There is as much wonjo in Chiolu as there is here in Aliakoro. At least six people have died there. Almost everyone in Olumba's family is ill. Olumba himself will probably catch the illness.'

Wago's eyes flashed with happiness as he spoke. Nobody else moved. Wago continued talking.

'Chiolu is afraid. They have sent men to make us release Olumba from his oath.'

'How do you know this?' asked Ikechi.

'Ha! ha! ha!' Wago laughed again. 'I come to Chiolu every night. Eze Diali is also very ill and may die at any moment. That's true isn't it?'

Wezume and his men felt very uncomfortable. They left the reception hall and went outside to talk.

'Wago knows everything about Chiolu,' said one man.

'Yes,' Wezume replied. 'Let us be honest with Okehi and ask him to release Olumba from his oath.'

'But if we do that, Aliakoro will get the Pond of Wagaba,' said Ikechi.

'There is as much wonjo here as in Chiolu,' said Wezume. 'Ogbunabali must be angry with both villages. We must ask Okehi to release Olumba from his oath because there is so much illness in the two villages. If Olumba dies now, it may not be because of the Pond of Wagaba and his oath, but because of the wonjo.'

They returned to the reception hall and Wezume told Okehi what they had decided. He asked Okehi to release Olumba from his oath. But the elders of Aliakoro would not do so.

* * *

When Wezume and his men returned to Chiolu, he told the people what had happened. Everyone was happy to hear that the sickness was in Aliakoro. It meant that Ogbunabali was punishing both villages and not only Chiolu.

The elders still wanted Olumba released from his oath. So they sent more men to Aliakoro to ask Okehi to release him. The Chief refused once again.

Meanwhile, more people died in both villages. Fewer and fewer elders went to meetings. Most of them were too sick to go. They stayed in their compounds and waited to die.

SIXTEEN

THE DEATH OF NYOMA

The people of Chiolu felt they were living in one large grave. They thought that if they lay down they would die.

One night, Nyoma went to Olumba's room.

'Olumba, my husband,' she said. 'Your daughter is very ill.'

Olumba jumped out of bed and went into Nyoma's room. Olumba's daughter was lying on the bed. Her little body was wet and cold. Olumba picked her up in his arms. He looked at his wife. She understood what his look meant. His little daughter was dead.

Nyoma began to cry loudly. Olumba held her in his arms.

'Crying will not bring her back to life,' he said kindly. 'People are dying everywhere. I'll go and tell Eze Diali.'

Olumba arrived at Diali's compound and met Chituru's eldest son.

'What's the matter?' Olumba asked.

'My father is dead,' answered the boy. He stood there with tears in his eyes.

'And how are you?' the boy asked Olumba.

'My daughter is dead.'

They both woke up the chief. He knew why they had come before they told him.

'Who is it this time?' Diali asked.

'My daughter.'

'And Chituru, my father.'

Suddenly, Eze Diali felt very lonely. Chituru, his most important elder, was dead.

'Wash their bodies and get them ready to be buried,' he said. 'I'll send gravediggers to make their graves.'

Chituru was buried later that day. As he had been a very

important elder, the ikoro sounded to call people to the funeral. Only a few people went. Those who did not go were either too ill or too sad.

Olumba went back to his compound. Nyoma was trying to cook a meal for the children. She was very thin and she was shivering.

'Nyoma, what is wrong?' Olumba asked.

'Nothing,' she replied. Suddenly she sat down and began to cry. Heavy tears ran down her cheeks.

'Crying cannot bring back our daughter,' Olumba said.

He got up silently to leave Nyoma and then he saw a small body in wrappers lying behind her. It was his son, Nchelem. Olumba knew why Nyoma was crying. Nchelem had the sickness, wonjo.

Olumba was now afraid again. A few days before, he had felt happier. He had thought that Ogbunabali was punishing the people in both villages. But his son was ill now. Olumba knew that Ogbunabali still thought him a special person.

That night, Olumba did not sleep. He got up before dawn and went outside. He looked at the sky. In a few days' time there would be a new moon and the six months would be over.

'I won't die before the six months are over,' Olumba said happily to himself.

'Yes, you will.'

It was the voice again. He had not heard it for a long time.

'I don't care if I do die,' Olumba heard himself say quietly.

'Your son, Nchelem, will die too,' said the voice.

'Many people have lost their sons,' replied Olumba.

'But you have only one son,' answered the voice.

Olumba bit his lips together and went back to bed, but he felt he was not alone. He rushed out and woke up his wives.

'I want to see Nchelem,' he said.

'He is here,' said Nyoma.

Olumba sat down beside his son until daylight came. Then he went to see Eze Diali.

The Chief was a little better. He still coughed, but he felt stronger.

'My son is ill,' said Olumba.

Diali did not answer. He just looked at Olumba.

'My son is sick,' Olumba said again.

Diali stood up and asked Olumba to follow him. They went into a room with four children in it. All the children were sick. Diali quickly shut the door and they both returned to the reception hall.

'It is different for you, my lord,' said Olumba. 'You have many sons but I have only one.'

'I have nothing to say,' answered Diali.

'What kind of world is this?' asked Olumba sadly.

'It is a world of the dead and the dying,' Diali replied. He bit his teeth together in anger and sadness.

Olumba walked home like a man walking in a dream.

*   *   *

Slowly Olumba felt himself becoming more ill, but he did not tell anyone in the village. In the end he spoke to his wife.

'I believe I have got it.'

'Wonjo?' said Nyoma.

'Yes.'

That night, Nyoma suddenly felt very ill. Her body became as hot as burning coals. Wogari went to Olumba.

'It's Nyoma,' she said. 'Come quickly.'

Olumba got up and went into Nyoma's room. He took his wife in his arms.

'Nyoma, please don't die,' he said quietly.

Nyoma smiled at her husband. The smile froze on her lips. She was dead.

Olumba seemed to go mad. He shouted and roared. No one came to see him. He looked at Nyoma's dead body, at his sick children and at Wogari.

He sat down and suddenly he fell asleep. Wogari stayed beside him and she too soon fell asleep.

SEVENTEEN

THE RETURN HOME

Nyoma was buried in the evening. Olumba was waving his arms about like a madman and talking nonsense.

That same night one of Eze Diali's sons died.

Ikechi went to see Olumba. He sat talking with him, trying to comfort him. Then he said goodnight to Olumba and went home.

On the way home, Ikechi saw two figures coming towards him in the darkness. He was a little frightened, but he stood still as the two figures came nearer. He thought that they were two old women on their way to see Diali.

'Who are you and who is dead?' Ikechi asked in a quiet voice. 'Is that Ikechi's voice?' one of the women said. 'Yes, I am Ikechi. Where are you going at this time of night?'

'Home,' the second woman said. 'Ikechi, take us home. We have travelled a long way without a man to help us.'

Ikechi went nearer to the two women.

'Who are you?' he asked.

'Chisa and Oda,' the other woman said.

Ikechi could not believe it. He looked more closely at the two women. Then he took them both tightly in his arms.

He shouted out loud with joy, but nobody came to see what was happening. Everyone was so used to cries and shouts in the night that they no longer took any notice.

Ikechi ran excitedly towards Diali's compound.

The ikoro boomed out, giving the village the happiest news it had heard for many, many months.

Ikechi knocked loudly at Olumba's door.

'Olumba! Wogari! Wake up! Oda is home again!' he shouted.

There was no answer.

Suddenly Ikechi felt afraid. How awful it would be if Olumba were dead!

Ikechi knocked again, this time more gently. Wogari opened the door. When she saw Oda, she took several steps backwards and trembled with fright.

'Oda! Oda!' she cried.

'Wogari!'

Wogari took Oda in her arms.

At first Olumba did not seem to understand what was happening. He opened his eyes slowly. When he saw Oda, he suddenly seemed to get much better. Oda embraced him and cried with joy. Ikechi left them alone.

'Where is my son, Nchelem?' Oda asked, after a while.

'He's lying here beside me.'

'Let me hold him,' she said.

'He is sick. Let him sleep now,' replied Olumba.

Oda told Olumba her story.

Oda and Chisa had been bought by two men. The men had later become sick and died. The women had walked to the river and found a boat.

'How did you find your way?' Olumba asked.

'A kind woman told us.'

'So those men died, too,' said Olumba. 'Ogbunabali is working everywhere, not only in Chiolu and Aliakoro. What a powerful god he is! Never before has a god punished a whole clan. How sad the Erekwi is now!'

Olumba took Oda in his arms and held her tightly.

'What about the . . . about the child?' Olumba asked, looking at his wife.

'Dead.'

'Was it a boy or a girl?'

'It was a boy.'

Olumba asked her no more questions.

'It is enough that you are here,' he said. He pointed to little Nchelem.

'Look after him if I die,' Olumba said quietly.

* * *

In the morning, Ikechi jumped out of bed, washed his face and ran to Diali's house to see Chisa. There were so many people in the house to welcome her that they could not be alone.

But in the evening they were together and they talked for a long time. Ikechi was very happy, but Chisa did not smile.

Ikechi tried to cheer her up.

Chisa started crying. Ikechi took her in his arms.

'What's wrong?' he asked.

'I can't marry you, Ikechi.'

'You can't marry me? Why not?'

Chisa cried and cried. It seemed that she would never stop.

'I tried to stop the man,' she said at last. 'Believe me, I did my best. I slapped him and I bit him. I told him I would kill myself. But he left his three wives and came after me. He was a big strong man. What could I do?'

Ikechi bit his teeth together.

'Is that all?' he asked.

'Yes.'

'Come here,' said Ikechi gently. Chisa went to him and Ikechi took her in his arms and embraced her.

EIGHTEEN

OLUMBA IS ATTACKED

The next day, Ikechi went to see Olumba.

'I may not be able to come and see you again,' he said.

'I know. I shall probably die in a day or two,' said Olumba quietly.

'That's not what I mean,' answered Ikechi.

'What do you mean then?'

'After I had buried my father yesterday, I felt ill. I think I have wonjo.'

Olumba said nothing.

'How do you feel when you have wonjo?' Ikechi asked.

'It's hard to say,' Olumba replied, coughing badly.

Ikechi stood up to leave. At the entrance to Olumba's compound, he met Wago, the Leopard-killer. Wago laughed when he saw that Ikechi was surprised.

'Wago!' Ikechi exclaimed.

'Yes. I am Wago, the Leopard-killer.'

'Why have you come to Chiolu?' asked Ikechi.

'I am here to greet my friends,' Wago answered. 'How is Olumba? I hear he is very sick.'

Ikechi said nothing. He ran to see Olumba.

'Wago, the Leopard-killer, is here!' he shouted.

Olumba immediately became very angry.

'Is he in my compound?' he asked.

'Yes, he's near the entrance.'

'Wago wants to know if I am dead, doesn't he?' asked Olumba. 'Then I won't die. I won't die before the new moon.'

Ikechi left Olumba alone and ran to tell the news to Diali. The Chief did not seem surprised.

'I know Wago has been walking round the village,' he said.

'Is he still thinking about the Pond of Wagaba?' asked Ikechi.

'Yes, my son.'

'But there is wonjo in Aliakoro and many people are dying there too.'

'That's true. But Wago is a strange man,' said Diali.

Ikechi ran home and collected his matchet. He went to find two of his friends and the three of them went to find Wago. But Wago had gone.

Many people went to see Olumba when they heard that Wago had been in his compound.

'We shall not let Aliakoro take the Pond of Wagaba. It is ours,' they said.

'Yes, men of Chiolu, the pond is ours. I shall not die,' answered Olumba.

'You will not die,' the villagers repeated.

'No, I shall not die,' answered Olumba.

The next day Olumba was feeling much weaker.

'I shall not die,' he kept saying to himself.

'You will die.' It was the voice again.

'I shall not die.'

'You will die,' said the voice.

Olumba told himself that he would not die. But slowly he became weaker and weaker. He became more and more afraid. When he was in bed, he shouted like a madman and talked nonsense.

Wago walked quietly round Olumba's compound. He listened to what was happening inside Olumba's house.

One minute Olumba was very cold and the next minute he started to sweat.

'I shall not die,' he said to himself.

'You will die.' The voice had come back to answer him.

Olumba saw a dark shape by his bed.

'No, no, I shall not die,' he cried out.

'Of course you will die,' the dark shape replied. 'Perhaps you will die tonight.'

'Not tonight! Not tonight!' Olumba shouted.

He picked up his stick and hit at the dark shape. Then he opened the door and walked out.

'I shall not die! I shall not die!' he shouted.

*   *   *

The next night, the same shape stood near Olumba's bed. It kept saying, 'You will die,' and Olumba kept replying, 'I shall not die.'

Olumba got out of bed again. He picked up his stick.

'I am Olumba,' he shouted. 'Come for me, Wago. I can kill eight people like you.'

Olumba left his compound. He found it difficult to walk. He was shouting loudly. Some of the villagers followed him.

Olumba walked like a drunken man.

Suddenly a large shape jumped out of the bushes and knocked Olumba to the ground. A few seconds later, Ikechi and his friends saw Olumba struggling with a large animal. They ran closer.

'It's a leopard,' Ikechi shouted. 'It's a leopard!'

Ikechi looked at Olumba struggling with the animal. He was afraid to use his matchet. If he did, he might hurt Olumba as well as the animal. Olumba was holding on to the leopard very tightly.

Suddenly Ikechi jumped forward and attacked the animal. He held its neck as tightly as he could. He squeezed and squeezed its neck. His friends tried to take the back legs of the animal away from Olumba's body.

There was a loud scream as Ikechi's matchet made a big cut in the animal. It let Olumba go. Ikechi dug his matchet into the animal a second time. The animal screamed out in pain. It jumped free and disappeared. But the leopard skin was left behind.

NINETEEN

THE FIGHT FOR THE POND
OF WAGABA COMES TO AN END

The next day everyone met in the Chief's reception hall. They could not believe Ikechi had captured such a beautiful skin.

'There is only one man who could have done this,' said Diali.

'Wago, the Leopard-killer,' said three people at the same time.

Diali looked at the dried skin. There were two knife cuts in it.

'Were these cuts very deep?' he asked.

'Wago cannot live,' said Ikechi. 'Let's go and find him.'

That morning a search party of four men set out to try to find Wago. First they went to the place where Wago had attacked Olumba. From there, they followed a line of blood on the ground.

In the evening, the search party returned to Chiolu.

'Did you see anything?' asked the Chief.

'Yes, we saw Wago, the Leopard-killer.'

The crowd cried out excitedly when they heard Wago's name.

'Where?'

'By the Pond of Wagaba,' answered Ikechi.

Everyone was silent.

'What was he doing?' asked Diali.

'Nothing. He was dead.'

There was a long silence.

'Did you kill him?' asked Diali.

'He was already dead before we saw him.'

'Had he died from the wounds of the matchet?'

'We don't know. We found him in the water.'

'Tell Eze Diali about the terrible smile on Wago's face,' said one of the men.

'Yes, my lord,' said Ikechi. 'What frightened us most was the horrible smile on the dead man's face.'

'But you say he was dead,' said Diali.

'Yes, but there was a horrible smile on the face of the dead body.'

The crowd shouted in fright.

'He must have killed himself,' said Diali. He bit his teeth together in anger.

'If he killed himself, it is his own business,' said Ikechi.

'And it's our business, too,' said Diali. He looked unhappy and worried.

'What do you mean?'

'This is terrible news. Terrible news,' Diali shouted out.

'Why?' asked Ikechi.

'We have lost the Pond of Wagaba,' cried Eze Diali.

'But Olumba is not dead yet.'

'No.'

'Then why have we lost the Pond?' asked Ikechi.

'We cannot fish from a pond in which somebody has drowned himself. The gods would not let us,' replied the Chief.

'Perhaps he drowned himself by accident,' someone said.

That evening Diali and the other elders went to see the local dibia. They wanted to find out how Wago had died. Had he died from his wounds or had he drowned himself in the pond? The dibia told them that Wago had killed himself. He had not drowned by accident.

As they left the dibia's house, they saw the new moon. The six months were ended. Olumba was still alive, but Chiolu had lost the Pond of Wagaba. Wago had stopped the men of

Chiolu using the pond. But he had also stopped the men of Aliakoro using it. He had drowned himself in the pond and neither village could ever fish there again.

Eze Diali and his men hurried home. Near the village they heard a scream. Another person had died of wonjo.

*　　*　　*

Many people died that year and in the other villages of the Erekwi clan.

At the same time, people were dying all round the world. But the clan did not know this.

The sickness that the Erekwi called wonjo was the great influenza attack of 1918. Twenty million people died all over the world.

POINTS FOR UNDERSTANDING

CHAPTER ONE

1. Why did Olumba tell Ikechi to eat some food?
2. What did the men of Aliakoro plan to do at the Pond of Wagaba?
3. Why did Eze Diali want to capture some of the poachers?
4. Why was Olumba chosen as leader?

CHAPTER TWO

1. 'He says the pond belongs to us and not to Chiolu.' Who was 'he'? What pond was he talking about? Who were 'us'?
2. 'Who is this rude, stupid man?' asked Olumba. What was the prisoner's reply?
3. Why did Olumba stop being angry?
4. 'We're not thieves,' said the prisoner. What reason did he give?
5. Which prisoner escaped?

CHAPTER THREE

1. What was the name of the god 'who kills by night'?
2. How long did Eze Diali say the Pond of Wagaba had belonged to Chiolu?
3. Olumba agreed to sell the prisoners back for five hundred manillas if the men of Aliakoro would agree to do something. What did they have to agree to do?
4. What was Wago's reply to Olumba?
5. The men of Aliakoro left Chiolu without saying good-bye. What do you think this meant?

CHAPTER FOUR

1. What did Ikechi see at the Pond of Wagaba?
2. Why was Olumba angry with Oda, his youngest wife?
3. Olumba divided his men into three groups. What was Olumba's plan?
4. Why did Olumba's plan not succeed?
5. Why did Elendu want to go to Chiolu to finish the fight?

CHAPTER FIVE

1. Why did Oda sleep in a room by herself?
2. How many women were taken prisoner?
3. Why did the men of Aliakoro allow Elendu to take the women with him?
4. Why was Olumba unable to follow the men of Isiali?
5. Why did the capture of Oda make Olumba miserable and unhappy?

CHAPTER SIX

1. Who was Nchelem and who was going to look after him?
2. Why had Ikechi not slept?
3. 'One woman is equal to one man.' How did Wago show that this was true?
4. Why were the men of Aliakoro unable to sell back the woman?

CHAPTER SEVEN

1. What was unusual about the way Okehi's son caught the two birds?
2. Why was Okehi unhappy and frightened?
3. Igwu said: 'Ali, the god of the earth is angry.' Why was Ali angry?
4. Which woman did Okehi have to give back to Aliakoro in order to please Ali?
5. What had happened to Oda and Chisa?

CHAPTER EIGHT

1. Olumba did not appear at the meeting to exchange the prisoners. Why was Wago worried when he noticed this?
2. What had happened at Aliakoro while the meeting was taking place?
3. Why did Wago become more important in Aliakoro?
4. Why did the Chiefs of the Erekwi clan decide to call a meeting? Who did they invite to the meeting?

CHAPTER NINE

1. At the meeting, one Chief said: 'We must let the gods decide.' How was this to be done?
2. Who was Ogbunabali and why was everyone afraid of him?
3. What would happen to Olumba if the Pond of Wagaba did not belong to Chiolu?
4. What promise was the Chief of Aliakoro asked to make?
5. Olumba had to take great care to avoid all danger. What arrangements did the villagers make in order to help him?

CHAPTER TEN

1. Why was Olumba bored?
2. Why did Olumba fall from the ladder?
3. Anwuanwu said to the men of Chiolu: 'I knew you were coming.' Why were Anwuanwu's words strange?
4. Who was hurting Olumba?

CHAPTER ELEVEN

1. 'Can a dibia be more powerful than a god?' asked Ikechi. What was Anwuanwu's reply?
2. Why did Wago go to visit Chiolu?
3. Why would Igwu have to try harder next time?

CHAPTER TWELVE

1. Why did Wago steal a piece of Olumba's wrapper?
2. Igwu threw a carved figure into the boiling pot. Who did the figure look like and what was Igwu trying to do?
3. Olumba began to hear something strange. What was it?
4. 'Anwuanwu looked at Olumba's wrapper and smiled.' Why did he smile?
5. Why did Anwuanwu leave many charms with Olumba?

CHAPTER THIRTEEN

1. Why did Eze Diali send out a search party to look for Oda and Chisa?
2. What news of Oda and Chisa did Ikechi bring back to Chiolu?
3. What story was Ikechi to tell Olumba about Oda and Chisa?
4. Ikechi wished that the pond of Wagaba had never belonged to Chiolu. Why?

CHAPTER FOURTEEN

1. Why did Olumba not go to look for the missing women?
2. What did Olumba ask Ogbunabali to do?
3. Why did everyone in Chiolu suddenly become frightened?
4. What did the people of Chiolu want the elders to do?
5. What did Olumba say to the people?

CHAPTER FIFTEEN

1. What did the men of Chiolu notice as they came near to Aliakoro?
2. What name did the people of Aliakoro give to the sickness which was attacking their village?
3. At first, Wezume did not ask Eze Okehi to release Olumba from his oath. What change did Wezume make in his words to Eze Okehi and why did he make this change?
4. Wago laughed at Wezume. Why?
5. If Olumba died because of the sickness, what would everyone believe?

CHAPTER SIXTEEN

1. 'Olumba knew that Ogbunabali still thought him a special person.' Why was Olumba certain of this?
2. Olumba began to hear the strange voice again. What did the voice say to him?
3. Olumba said to Eze Diali: 'It is different for you, my lord.' What was the difference?
4. What happened to Olumba when Nyoma died?

CHAPTER SEVENTEEN

1. What happy news did the ikoro give to the village?
2. Why did Olumba say that Ogbunabali was working everywhere?
3. Why did Chisa think that she could not marry Ikechi?
4. What was Ikechi's answer to Chisa's fears?

CHAPTER EIGHTEEN

1. Although many people in both villages were dying, Wago was thinking about something else. What was he thinking about?
2. What did the dark shape keep saying to Olumba?
3. 'But the leopard skin was left behind.' Who had attacked Olumba?

CHAPTER NINETEEN

1. How did Wago stop the people of both villages fishing in the Pond of Wagaba?
2. What was 'wonjo'?

GLOSSARY

SECTION ONE

Comparisons

Writers often compare one thing with another to make a description seem more interesting and more real. Such comparisons often begin with 'like' or 'as', and they are called *similes*. The following is a list of similes used in this book.

body (page 49) like Olumba's body
broomstick (page 57) as thin as a broomstick
coals (page 66) as hot as burning coals
dream (page 66) like a man walking in a dream
elastic (page 9) like elastic
elephant (page 3) as much noise as an elephant
madman (pages 18 and 74) like a madman
man (page 75) like a drunken man
rivers (page 50) like little rivers
thunder (page 62) like a crash of thunder
tunnel (page 6) like walking through a dark tunnel
wind (page 16) like the wind
woman (page 3) like an old woman

SECTION TWO

Terms to do with magic and religion

Olumba has *to swear by a god*. In front of everyone, Olumba has to say that something is true. If it is true, the god will let him live. But if it is not true, the god will kill him This swearing by a god is called an *oath*. Later, the villagers become afraid and they want Olumba released from his oath. They want to ask the god to forget about the oath altogether.

cowries (page 43)
    seashells used by a dibia to tell the past and the future.

god – to swear by the name of god (page 36)
>   see note on page 86.

image (page 37)
>   a wooden figure cut to look like a god.

oath – to release from an oath (page 58)
>   see note on page 86.

priest (page 37)
>   a man who attends to the needs of a god.

sacrifices (page 15)
>   something given to please a god – often an animal is killed
>   and given to the god.

shrine (page 37)
>   the place where a god is worshipped.

spirit (page 37)
>   the villagers believed that everyone had a body which you can
>   see and a spirit which cannot be seen.

swear – to swear by a god (page 13)
>   see note on page 86.

SECTION THREE

Terms to do with local life and customs

clan (page 3)
>   the people of a number of villages who followed the same
>   customs and spoke the same language.

compound (page 3)
>   a high wall was built round the huts of each family in a
>   village. The land inside the wall was called the compound.

ikoro (page 15)
>   a hollow wooden gong. Different noises were used to give
>   news to the villagers and to call them to meetings.

manillas (page 12)
>   metal rings which were worn on the arm and were also used
>   as money.

matchet (page 4)
>   a large, heavy knife.

nuts – kola nuts (page 12)
>   when guests arrived in a village or in a compound, kola nuts
>   were broken and a piece given to everyone present. The

people ate these pieces together to show that they were all friends.

slaves (page 31)

a slave was a man or woman who was not free. A slave was owned by another person.

wrappers (page 43)

large pieces of cloth used to cover the body.

SECTION FOUR

Terms expressing emotion through body movements

bit – bit his lips together (page 23)

a strong feeling of sadness and of anger made Olumba bite his lips together.

bit – bit his teeth together (page 23)

a strong feeling of anger and disappointment made Olumba bite his teeth together.

jumped – his heart jumped (page 15)

Ikechi felt a sudden, strong feeling of fear.

throat – a lump came into his throat (page 53)

Ikechi felt a strong feeling of love and sadness.

SECTION FIVE

General

killer – leopard-killer (page 8)

a leopard is a strong, fierce animal with a yellow and brown spotted skin. It is a very dangerous animal and difficult to kill. A man who is called a leopard-killer must be very strong and brave.

massage (page 20)

to rub someone's body with your hands in order to take away pain.